A Day of Grace

Daily insights for spritiual reflection
Michael Lightweaver

Mountain Light Publishing
PO Box 18909
Asheville, NC. 28814

ISBN 0-9666414-0-X

To all those whose love has
touched my life...

You know who you are, but will
probably never realize the
important role you have played
on my journey.

Introduction

These insights were originally received as personal guidance. I was subsequently asked to put them in to the present form of daily reflections, as a book of meditations.

It was also suggested that they were to be arranged according to the ancient moon calendar of twenty eight days. This brings us into attunement with the natural rhythm of the Earth and returns us to a consciousness of the cyclical nature of time.

A table of new moon dates can be found in the back of the book. You may follow day by day, beginning with the new moon, or simply open the book at random and let it speak to you in that manner. Either way, you are encouraged to use them as a companion to your meditations for a full year. The information is of value only to the extent that it is integrated into the core of one's being. Integration occurs over a period of months or years through reflection and practice.

Jesus said, "You will know a tree by its fruit." Accept

them only if they speak to your heart. It is my hope that you would not reject them because they were "channeled" nor be awed and accept them without question for the same reason. It is not the alleged source, but the message that is important in any supposed channeling. The ultimate test is how any information resonates with the deepest part of your own knowing - your heart.

The essence of the message is Love - so simple yet so profound. It is the one thing which unites us across the many chasms we have built with our politics, religions and philosophies. Those who integrate Love - Divine Grace that is without judgement, fear or blame - into their lives, are of one nature and a common faith. Our pathway to the Divine is the heart where Love reigns. It is not the mind paved with dogma and beliefs.

My wish for you is that these insights will inspire you on your own spiritual journey and that today, for you, may be a day of grace.

Michael Lightweaver
Mountain Light Sanctuary

DAY ONE

KODOISH, KODOISH, KODOISH, ADONAI 'TSEBAYOTH.
KODOISH, KODOISH, KODOISH, ADONAI 'TSEBAYOTH.
KODOISH, KODOISH, KODOISH, ADONAI 'TSEBAYOTH.

So it is we are here in the full presence and in the full power, we the emissary of The Unutterable, we the emissary of Divine Presence, we the emissary of The Great Mystery, we the emissary of the I AM that I AM.

We come to you in love. We come to you in the fullness of the glory of the Presence. We come to you in a blinding ray of light that illuminates all darkness, that dissolves all shadows, that enlightens all ignorance, that dissolves all fear.

We come to you in light, we come to you in love, we come to you in truth. We come to you from beyond the edge of infinity and eternity. We come to you from the innermost realms of your own heart ... and we lift you, we lift you up. We lift you up into the seventh heaven, into resonance with the macrocosm. We lift you into the realm of pure joy, of pure ecstasy, into the Presence of the I AM that I AM. In this realm of pure delight and ecstasy, we see the shadows of ignorance dissolving within you at a cellular level. We see the heavy veil over your eyes dissolving as you come to understand the true nature of being.

In this realm of the Unutterable, we grant you a deed to your own heart. For you have been as a landless serf paying homage to the lords of fear, to the lords of judgment, to the lords of death and disease, to the lords of pain and suffering, to the lords who have ruled your species for eons.

Now in this realm of bliss, this realm of joy, this realm of ecstasy, we grant you a deed, a title free and clear to your own heart. We call you to step away from service to the lords of illusion and to take possession of your own dwelling, granted to you free and clear. The time has come to become the lord of your own manor, to dwell in truth, to dwell in light, to dwell in love, to dwell in the heart of the I AM that I AM. It is the land of magic. It is the land of miracles.

In this land of sunshine all things will prosper. The days of toil, the days of suffering, the days of darkness in service to the lords of illusion are of the past. In this land of light, love, joy and bliss, all things will prosper. In this land of eternal spring, the fragrance of new life will ever fill the air.

This land of delight, which is your own, has always been here for you, waiting, languishing. It has been waiting for its master to awaken from the dark dream. It has been waiting for the Fisher King to discover the Grail.

The time is NOW. The Fisher King has awakened from the dark dream, and the land has awakened and will flourish. The Grail has been restored to its most sacred altar. Know this, you are a son of God who has suffered long from the amnesia of your identity. Your years of slavery to the lords of illusion are over. You have returned to reclaim your rightful title, to reclaim the chalice.

The blessings of El Shadai, the God who is more than enough, will flow ceaselessly. A river of light will flow out of the land of Zion from the heart of the New Jerusalem, nourishing the whole of your species.

We are an emissary of the I AM that I AM. We go.

DAY TWO

KODOISH, KODOISH, KODOISH, ADONAI TSEBAYOTH.
KODOISH, KODOSIH, KODOISH, ADONAI TSEBAYOTH.
KODOSIH, KODOISH, KODOISH, ADONAI TSEBAYOTH.

It is critical that you move forward with us now into this new phase of co-creativity. There is a larger plan which you do not yet see clearly, but you feel it at a gut level. It is critical, as you move forward step by step, to work in cooperation with divine guidance. We see from the macrocosm, the big picture. Your circuits are not yet developed sufficiently to handle the totality so we give it to you bit by bit until you can handle more.

As you work with true guidance, all will move forward in accordance with the plan. But you always have choice, for this is a planet of choice. As you choose to surrender totally to guidance, all unfolds for you in pure joy. Remember this, there is a season for everything.

If there is ever a question about the authenticity of any plan, project or person, the criteria for evaluation is love. Ask yourself, "What is the love quotient of this project, plan, or person?" The yardstick is always love, whether for situations, plans, projects or people, or when you look deeply into your own heart. The final question is, "Is this arising from the wellspring of love or fear? From love or power? From love or ego? From love or greed? Where love is, Divine Presence is. Where love is truly, fear cannot dwell. Where love is, protection is impeccable. Be therefore as wise as serpents and as innocent as doves.

Underlying all is the energetic pattern of your planet and each entity. Each energetic pattern vibrates at a frequency and resonates with frequencies similar to its own. This is the science behind the universal law of attraction: Like Attracts Like.

When we say that love is your protection, we are not speaking of spiritual platitudes, but of universal scientific law. When you dwell in fear, you attract fear-based energies. Fear of attack is the very source of attack. Resistance creates opposition. When you refine and increase your own vibrations in the higher frequencies of love, you cannot be touched by the lower energies. For them, you do not exist. You have become invisible because you are no longer in their frequency range. It is critical to understand this and to continually work on increasing the frequencies of your own energy. This is your source - your only source - of "protection."

We close by reminding you to continue to refine your own energy, physically, mentally, emotionally, and spiritually. Surrender more and more to the current of Divine Grace and allow it to flow through you and emanate from you. You are participating in a co-creative process as creation moves through this transition. This should be a joy born of love, not a pain born of fear. It can only be so collectively as it is individually, and you are responsible for no one but yourself in this matter. Your doings are only important in the context of the dream. Ultimately it is the "who" of your being and not the "what" of your doing that will transform the world.

We are complete for now.

DAY THREE

KODOISH, KODOISH, KODOISH, ADONAI TSEBAYOTH.
KODOISH, KODOISH, KODOISH, ADONAI TSEBAYOTH.
KODOISH, KODOISH, KODOISH, ADONAI TSEBAYOTH.

You have been brought into resonance this morning for gaining greater understanding of your role and purpose at this moment in your Earth's history. It is essentially a matter a being rather than doing . There will be doing - much doing - but this will be a vehicle for the beingness which will be the true transformative aspect of what you are about. Do you understand?

Your key word at this time is resonance. Manifestation is contingent upon resonance. That which you wish to create you must come into resonance with. The same is true with people. If there are those with whom you are to work, lead or influence, first come into resonance with them or a given situation. It is only then that you can gently guide in a certain direction. Be cautious however of manipulation. All should be done toward the highest good, in love and not in ego.

Everything operates on a frequency and has its own signature vibration. This is true for individuals, organizations, events and even situations. Your role is to be a "frequency modulator." This is what we mean about the importance of "being" as opposed to "doing." For purposes of illustration, let us say that everything vibrates between a frequency of 1 and 100. The actual frequencies are different, but we are not speaking scientifically here, only for the purposes of easy illustration.

Love is the highest frequency. Pure love is the total absence of judgment and fear. To increase your frequency requires the neutralization of judgment. There is a difference between judgment and discernment, however. Discernment is an evaluation of what is in the best interest of all concerned or what is for the highest good. Judgment on the other hand involves blame. These are the key criteria for understanding whether you are exercising judgment or discernment.

Back to our point. Your personal role is to be a frequency modulator. The reason you are being prompted to spend more time alone is for the purpose of increasing your own frequency. It is not possible for you to do this when you are so immersed and influenced by the global thought-form. This consensus reality is no more than the collective dream of humanity - the great illusion.

You are being called apart in order to awaken and to clarify your energy. To clarify means to see clearly. As you began to see with more clarity, judgment will dissolve. As judgment dissolves, your discernment will become more keen. This judgment must first dissolve within yourself about yourself. You cannot be free of judgment of others until you have become free of judgment of self. As judgment dissolves, the frequency of love increases. As love increases, you become pure of heart and return to innocence. You "become as little children." When this happens, you become a frequency modulator and, with each situation or circumstance you enter, you bring change by your very presence, not by what you do or say. This is the true purpose of what you are to be about at this time. All else is just an excuse to put you there.

We are complete.

DAY FOUR

KODOISH, KODOISH, KODOISH, ADONAI TSEBAYOTH.
KODOISH, KODOISH, KODOISH, ADONAI TSEBAYOTH.
KODOISH, KODOSIH, KODOISH, ADONAI TSEBAYOTH.

Yes, we are here once again at your invitation. We are the emissary of the Universal Divine Light Council. We come to you in response to your soul invitation. We come now because the speed at which things are moving requires our presence and introduction. Many things which we have told you in the past are now lost to your conscious mind; but there is a remembrance at the inner level of the soul.

You have arrived at the beginning point of a new phase. You do not have an inkling of the depth or profundity of what is about to take place. The only thing we can tell you at this point is to live in a continual and complete state of surrender. There are things which will occur that you will not understand but, be assured, it is all in divine order. You have reached a point of inner clarification and resonance in which every act, person and situation will be specific to that to which you are to be about. Nothing is by accident.

All things are essential props in your drama, but all

are not helpful. Therefore we give you a technique to validate each person, circumstance or situation which arises. Send out an energy probe from your solar plexus and touch into the energy of that person, situation or idea. You will immediately get a reading of it which will register as a positive or negative. All this means is that the person, situation or idea is appropriate to you and your work at this moment or not. It does not represent a judgment of good or bad, just an evaluation of appropriateness at this moment for you.

We are an emissary of the Universal Divine Light Council. We are here to offer guidance, understanding and assistance. The so called human, ego-dominated part of your self, which extends into third-dimensional reality, is actually just a fraction of the YOU. It is but a tiny microsystem with limited range and ability. However, to the extent that you come into resonance with the I AM, we can work through you. We can utilize your energy, presence and skills in helping to bring the Divine Plan into fulfillment on Earth. This can only be done when you surrender your own ego and its little dramas to the designs of love. In your surrender, or better stated, in your alignment, you will be totally provided for in joy in all ways, physically, emotionally and spiritually. Know that this surrendering or being in alignment is an ongoing moment by moment process. It is not a one-time event.

We are complete

DAY FIVE

KODOISH, KODOISH, KODOISH, ADONAI TSEBAYOTH.
KODOISH, KODOISH, KODOISH, ADONAI TSEBAYOTH.
KODOISH, KODOISH, KODOISH, ADONAI TSEBAYOTH.

Morning has arrived , the morning of a new day, the morning of a new Earth. This is the time of the fulfillment. It is that time which is spoken of in the Bible as the separation of the sheep and the goats.

Not so long ago, everyone was facing west, still looking in the direction of the dying light which so long ago disappeared from your planet. The light has made its full circle and has returned. There are those of you now who have turned your backs on the darkness of the past and are seeing the glimmer of light in the east. There are more and more of you, but most people are still facing west. The masses are captivated by the global thought-form of fear and distress born of judgment and blame. Movement is now underway. Where you once stood together and simply faced different directions, you are now beginning to move. Some will move toward the rising sun and some toward the dying night; some toward love and some toward fear.

Do not be tricked. The movement toward the east, toward the light, is not about the reading of new-age books or involvement in new or old philosophies. It is not about the reviving of the lost knowledge of Atlantis. There was much in those lost continents that is well to leave beneath the waters. The ancient ways, the new science which is coming from beyond your planet, are but technologies which will help ground those of the east in the new reality which is coming into being.

Do not be tricked. That which divides the people of the east and the west is the choice of Love over Fear. You may be surprised to find that there are those whom you consider leaders of new consciousness who, when you look closely, are facing west. They are locked into the global thought-form of fear, while wearing the robes of the new age. Likewise, you will find those whom you consider of an old conscious-ness, who resonate with love at the core of their beings. They may have little intellectual information about new-age things, and yet they are facing the east, radiating and reflecting the rising sun. So do not be in judgment.

Live a simple, quiet, discerning life. Allow the rising sun to fill your mind and heart. Purify your spirit and nourish your soul. Be ready to embrace all who turn from the west to the east as they feel the warmth of the rising sun at their backs, but know that those who remain in fear are there by soul choice. Those in fear will not always be in fear, but they will be there for a time as even you have been. Let today be a day of light. Move into a deeper level of consciousness, a deeper level of resonance. You are integrating into the light. Once you have come into a greater and more complete resonance, we will give you instructions as to your next step.

So be it. We are complete.

DAY SIX

KODOISH, KODOISH, KODOISH, ADONAI 'TSEBAYOTH.
KODOISH, KODOISH, KODOISH, ADONAI 'TSEBAYOTH.
KODOISH, KODOISH, KODOISH, ADONAI 'TSEBAYOTH.

We have invited you into resonance this morning and into the garden of joy to have a dialog with you. You are moving now into a deeper level of resonance in order to integrate your being more fully into the greater whole. We are working with your energy pattern even now as you read, altering certain outdated circuits. We are adjusting your frequency in order that you may more fully accept that which is being initiated in your life at this time.

Remember, move through each day, moment by moment in a state of surrender and deference to Divine Will, which is love. Always look to the light for direction and guidance and you will not falter. Your path will be a path of joy and delight. Your life will be a statement of love. As you continue to grow in love, your frequency will increase, and you will be able to release all judgment and see the core of innocence in all. There is neither good nor evil; only appropriateness or inappropriateness. You are being immersed in showers of divine bliss and blessings. Duality is being unified in your being. You are anchoring in truth and power and, from this place, you will move forward.

We are moving you into deeper levels of awareness and understanding and anchoring you in the solid rock of Divine Presence which is manifested in Love. Your world is on a collision course with Light; a light that is so powerful, so profound, that it will be intolerable to some. There are those who will find in it instant illumination - in a twinkling. Others will find it to be a searing fire which will utterly destroy their illusions of duality and crack their dramas wide open.

You have been called apart at the same time that you are being sent forth. You are becoming anchored in Divine Presence. It is from this anchoring that you are to go forth as an emissary of Divine Presence and as a messenger of Light. The message you carry will not be what you say or do, but the energy you bear. It is this energy that is being refined.

Work in resonance with divine guidance and everything will flow smoothly. It is no longer necessary to swim upstream as you have so often done in the past.

We are complete.

DAY SEVEN

KODOISH, KODOISH, KODOISH, ADONAI TSEBAYOTH.
KODOISH, KODOISH, KODOISH, ADONAI TSEBAYOTH.
KODOISH, KODOISH, KODOISH, ADONAI TSEBAYOTH.

You have invoked and called forth the presence of Love; the presence of the emissary of the Universal Divine Light Council. We come.

We come in resonance. We are working with you and

endeavoring diligently to move you from where you have been to where you are going. We are birthing you from one state of being into another state of being.

During this birthing process, there is a certain amount of stress that you may experience, but this will soon be completed. You are both the baby and mother. In both instances, the easiest way for you to move through this birthing comfortably is to surrender, to relax and to let go. The more you can breathe into this experience and accept it, the easier it will be.

There are loving hands on the other side waiting for you. There are teachers, guides, angels and archangels waiting for you as you leave the womb. You are awakening, emerging from the dark dream and being birthed into a new broader reality. It will not be easy to speak of this to others.

You are wanting this birthing process to be completed very quickly, but do not be in a hurry. Everything is being carefully arranged. Let today be a day of joy. Let today be a day of love. Let today be a day as if it were your last. Live each day, now, as if it were the last ... no tomorrow ... no yesterday.

What is your work today? It is to adjust your perception. It is not necessary to manipulate the circumstances in which you find yourself but simply work on your perception. Allow yourself to be more deeply in resonance with Love, with the I AM that you are. Awaken to the joy of the I AM that I AM.

We place upon you hands of light. We place upon you the healing hands of love. We place upon you the hands of joy. We surround you with the light of love and protection. With the sunshine of Divine Presence we bless you this day. Be patient. All things are unfolding according to the Divine Plan and divine wisdom. Stay awake, stay connected, and stay in love.

We are complete.

Day Eight

KODOISH, KODOISH, KODOISH, ADONAI TSEBAYOTH.
KODOISH, KODOISH, KODOISH, ADONAI TSEBAYOTH.
KODOISH, KODOISH, KODOISH, ADONAI TSEBAYOTH.

We remind you constantly to look at the message and not at the identity of the messenger. See if the message resonates with your heart. Listen with your heart to that which we have to say to you at this time.

We are an emissary of the Universal Divine Light Council. We come from far beyond the density of your third dimension. You are anchored, grounded - and for some, trapped - into a very small corner of your consciousness. There is some lingering anxiety and fear. Even as your heart moves into resonance, your gut is locked into the third dimensional illusion. In this tiny corner of your consciousness which dominates at a feeling level, there is a touch of fear and sadness.

It is as if your mind were trapped in your solar plexus. But what can we say to you? We say, as we have said again and again and again - surrender. Your source is El Shadai. Your source is not your employment or your investments. It is El Shadia, the God who is more than enough. The pathway to God is your heart. It is a moment by moment endeavor. It is a moment by moment challenge.

We come now to liberate you from the tininess of your perspective and into the fullness of the All That Is, I AM Presence. Step out of your self-imposed prison of consciousness with its bars of fear - the fear of loving, the fear of giving too much.

Step out into the light. Step into the presence of El Shadia, the presence of Adonai - the presence of Love. For in love there can be no fear. Allow that grace to permeate the very essence of your being. Allow it to fill your heart, your mind, your gut, your soul.

Call down that grace that it may fill, surround and interpenetrate the very essence of your being. Open your heart, open your arms, open your life and be filled to the brim with divine grace.

As you allow your vibrations to increase, every person who walks into your presence will be blessed by love and the fruit of that love which is joy.

Hands of light will bear you up and you will soar on the magic carpet of divine grace. So be it. We go.

DAY NINE

KODOISH, KODOISH, KODOISH, ADONAI TSEBAYOTH.
KODOISH, KODOISH, KODOISH, ADONAI TSEBAYOTH.
KODOISH, KODOISH, KODOISH, ADONAI TSEBAYOTH.

We are here, the emissary of the Universal Divine Light Council, and we are slightly amused at this internal struggle you are experiencing. You are quite good at communicating to others to be in a place of non-judgment, and yet you still hold so much judgment toward yourself.

You know you are your own worst enemy. Most people are. You have a deep and fundamental need to be in authenticity. It is this very need to be authentic that gives you your integrity but, to a certain extent, it also undermines you from completely coming in to the full power of who you are.

It is difficult to be locked into a small ego personality. It feels like a third-dimensional tight shoe. Understand - that which comes to you is a reflection of the universal consciousness of which you are a part. We say that we are an emissary of the Universal Divine Light Council but, the truth is, we are a part of yourself. We are not an entity which comes in to possesses your body. No, we are that part of you that is "tuned in" on a vibrational level with the higher frequencies of Light.

When you are fine-tuned to this wavelength, that which comes through will be very clear, very precise. Even though it is a reflection of your knowing, it is also coming from a place that is more open, more clear, more fluid than that part of you which normally speaks and is locked into a more limited perspective.

You are tapping into or tuning into that part of your consciousness which functions from the macrocosm, the big picture. Normally, you function on a day-to-day basis from the perspective of the microcosm, from the small picture of you, he, she, them, us.

We call you to tune into that vibrational level which is from the macrocosm. You may call it your higher self. We call it the Universal Divine Light Council. But, understand this, we are not an entity. We are a perspective. We are a vibrational level that is able to perceive things from a slightly different perspective than the ego-dominated part of yourself which normally functions in your day-to-day world.

Now you have entered a pathway that will carry you

further and further into this macrocosm. In the past, you operated from the microcosmic perspective 99% of the time. Each time you are in judgment, each time you are in blame, each time you buy into another persons condemnation or criticism of someone else, you are locking into the microcosmic perspective. Most people in your dimension are trapped in this perspective 100% of the time.

You know intellectually that there is this macrocosm, this big picture. We are inviting you to spend more and more of your time there. Each morning and each evening, come to a place of quietude within yourself. Tune into the macrocosm and view yourself, your circumstances, your world, your relationships, everything in your life from the big picture. As you do this more and more, your perspective will gradually be altered until you truly awaken and see clearly. You will see with the eyes of God.

There will come a time when it will not be necessary for you to communicate or be communicated with in the manner we are now doing. Channeled communication is a phenomenon of the microcosm because it creates a sense of separation. It leads you to believe that something outside of yourself is speaking to or through yourself. And of course, this is not the way it is at all.

As you move into resonance with the macrocosmic perspective, you will be in a state of continual communication, but not in words. You will be functioning at a fundamental level. You will become the macrocosm. Every moment, every thought, every action will function from this. You will not need to be instructed by it, you will function from it.

We have given you a deeper and greater understanding of this. You have set your foot upon this path and you will not turn around. Surrender, trust, release. You are surrounded by a host of angelic ones who will bear you up and enfold you with protection and blessings. You will be sustained in all ways ... physically, emotionally and spiritually.

We are complete.

Day Ten

KODOISH, KODOISH, KODOISH, ADONAI 'TSEBAYOTH.
KODOISH, KODOISH, KODOISH, ADONAI 'TSEBAYOTH.
KODOISH, KODOISH, KODOISH, ADONAI 'TSEBAYOTH.

We come, an emissary of the Universal Divine Light Council. We reiterate that we are not an entity but rather a frequency into which you tune according to your own vibration. We are an emissarial frequency of the Divine Light Council. We are a frequency into which you tune and from which are able to broadcast within the context of your own understanding and within your own manner of expression.

We are aware of the deep pain and sadness that you have experienced as it relates to the land of Jerusalem. Let us speak to what is transpiring in that place. Your planet is now experiencing the throes of tremendous change. Some of this is geological, but more of it is social.

Why Jerusalem? Why Jerusalem, you ask. The land of Jerusalem is like the center of a stage upon which the whole drama of humanity is taking place. The things which transpire in this land grab and hold the attention of the whole world. The same events which take place in this land could take place in other lands and fail to gain the notice of your global nervous system - the media.

Let us compare Earth to the human body which receives injuries. These injuries are registered in specific places. If you break your toe or cut your finger, these will register in those places. Some places which receive an injury will not get your attention as much as other places. There are also certain illnesses which will call your attention to the need for the overall healing of your body-mind-spirit, more than other illnesses. So, what happens in the land of Jerusalem as a focal point affects the whole planet. It calls attention not only to the pain, illnesses, tragedy and suffering of all humanity, but also to the need for healing.

There is an advance team, a "spiritual swat team," in place which has been in place for some time in that location - nearby. This team is working against great odds. It is critically important that they be supported in every possible way; mentally, emotionally, physically and particularly spiritually.

As the intensity of the drama unfolds with wave after wave of apparent chaos, which is in fact a part of the divine unfolding, there are those on the team whose trust and faith will fail. It is so easy to be caught up in the drama of "us" and "them" as if it were indeed reality. And so it is with yourselves. This drama in the land of Jerusalem and the work of these ones who bear light are but a microcosm of the drama unfolding on your planet and the ever present temptation of allowing your emotions to trap you into the illusion of separation.

Light teams such as these need the complete support of the family of Light throughout your world. There are many places and many teams such as these, but this place is a place upon which the eyes of the world are focused. What takes place here affects the global thought-form. This is the reason we ask you to devote what may seem like an inordinate amount of time and energy to the land of Jerusalem.

The land of Jerusalem is a major and an ancient portal into your earth. It is through this portal that many energies enter and leave. It is a gateway that has been battled over for eons, because those who control the gate to a large extent control that which ultimately occurs on your planet.

As you well know, the forces of chaos feed upon fear. The forces of chaos feed upon hatred. The energies of fear, anger and hatred are their food. They thrive upon it. It is with the illusion of separation that they perpetuate their supply, keeping alive old hatreds and creating new ones. In the face of love, non-judgment and forgiveness, they wither. They drift away in the wind.

It has been in the best interest of the forces of chaos to keep circumstances as such that there would be a constant struggle and fighting in order to create the necessary fear, anger and hatred upon which to feed. But what you are witnessing now in the land of Jerusalem are the death throes of what was. Very often in the last moments before death, there seems to be a burst of energy, and the person sits up and is very alert and filled with energy, only to pass a moment later.

You are seeing this moment now on the planet. It is the moment of dawn and the darkness is clinging in desperation to the night. It is also the moment of choice. Some will turn their backs to the rising sun, following the dying night. Some will face the east and awaken from the great nightmare, illuminated by the rising sun.

It is a time of the separation of the sheep and the goats. One people, walking toward the rising sun, faces radiant, immersed in the light of Divine Presence. Another people facing the west, following the dying night, holding onto the darkness and refusing to awaken from the nightmare. And it is a choice. It is a choice moment by moment that each of you makes in your heart. Every decision is a decision toward the dawn or toward the dying night. Every decision is to awaken to the reality of who you are, why you are here and what this is really about, or a decision to remain asleep, enthralled in the nightmare of duality, this nightmare of good and evil, of "them" and "us." This is the nightmare that has fed the forces of chaos for so long.

You are at a point of decision. This is not a one-time choice. It is a moment-by-moment choice every moment of your life. It is the choice to love or to fear. It is the choice to love or to hate. It is the choice to face a new day or the dying night. It is a choice to awaken or cling to the nightmare. The center-stage people in the land of Jerusalem see themselves in two warring camps. Within each group, there are the people of peace and those who clamor for war. So in one sense, the true division is not between Jews and Arabs. It is between those who are locked into hatred, anger, revenge and the ancient ways of the blood feud, regardless of their ethnic origin, and the people of peace. The people of peace know that this conflict cannot be solved in the ways of the past. If it could, it would have already been solved. If the solution could be found at the end of a gun, then the problem would have been solved long ago.

Yet let us speak here of another great danger. Duality is duality. You are tempted to be in a place of judgment and blame for those whom you see as extremists on both sides. You judge them to be wrong and the peacemakers to be right. Now within the context of the dream, the way of the peacemaker works. Those who reach out to build bridges over the abyss will bring about a healing. Those who pitch bombs at one another across the abyss, whether they are literal bombs, verbal bombs, or thought-form bombs, are making the abyss deeper and wider. This simply does not work to create what ultimately is the desire of each and every person in the land of Jerusalem ... the desire for peace, for justice, for security ... to raise their families in peace, justice and prosperity.

There is something more fundamental here, and this is where it is important for you to look within your own heart. Those who kill prime ministers, those who machine gun innocent worshippers in their mosque, those who blow themselves up and take innocent ones along with them in the most tragic manner - even these are innocent. At the core of their being they are innocent.

Can you accept that? Or are you yourself still trapped in the global thought-form and the great illusion of the nightmare of this third dimension in these latter days of transition?

We deliberately challenge you with this thought for we know that it difficult for you to accept it. We do it to point out to you the extent to which you are still asleep and caught up in the dream drama of duality, of judgment and blame. If you could see from the macrocosm as we do, you would understand. There will be a time when you will understand.

Know this, love and fear cannot occupy the same space. Love and judgment cannot occupy the same space. To the extent that you shelter fear, judgment and blame, there is no accommodation for love. Until your heart is totally given to and possessed by Love, you cannot be a true and perfect channel of Divine Presence. This is simply the way it works. Let all of the circumstances of your world, the dramas you see unfolding, be as metaphors for what is transpiring in your own life. Let them be lessons and guides. Let them help clarify your own understanding, choosing those thoughts and making those decisions which will gradually increase the frequency of your own spirit as you come into resonance with the oneness of Divine Presence.

We are an emissary of the Universal Divine light Council.

We go.

DAY ELEVEN

KODOISH, KODOISH, KODOISH, ADONAI 'TSEBAYOTH.
KODOISH, KODOISH, KODOISH, ADONAI 'TSEBAYOTH.
KODOISH, KODOISH, KODOISH, ADONAI 'TSEBAYOTH.

We are here, always as close to you as your own breath, we the emissary of the Universal Divine Light Council. You have embraced the ideas we have given you about the unity of life and about the oneness of the great I AM, and yet do you find this difficult to integrate into your experience? Do you find yourself falling back into old ways? We are offering an opportunity to integrate that which you are learning and remembering into your experience, so it will be that which you are.

It may, perhaps often, feel as you are swimming through honey. Know, however, that you are moving forward in spite of your impatience and your desire to fly. We know that you are of a sincere heart. The thickness of this honey that you are swimming through is your own intensity, your seriousness and yes, your heaviness. We invite you to lighten up!

How to lighten up? The more you surrender, the less

you will be carrying and the lighter you will be. The more you trust, the more rapidly you will move forward. Surrender those things you are carrying to those who are working and walking with you in spirit. They are here to help you. And know this; everything is being worked out in a good way at a level in which you are not directly involved from a conscious standpoint.

It is time for you to dance more, to sing, to celebrate the love of the great I AM. Come out of the wintertime of your experience. Come out of the wintertime of your spirit. Take off the heavy overcoat of fear and allow the sun's radiance to penetrate you. As you laugh, as you sing, as you dance, as you make music and celebrate the love of the Most Holy One you will move forward rapidly in life.

Now you have with you your guardians. You have with you your angels and archangels surrounding and traveling with you. They are giving you guidance and protection.

Go into a deep place of resonance. Be in resonance with who you are at the core of your being. Be in resonance with the angelic realms and the love of the I AM. All things will unfold in beauty and wonder for you to the extent that you are in resonance with the love of the I AM. So be it, we go.

DAY TWELVE

KODOISH, KODOISH, KODOISH, ADONAI 'TSEBAYOTH.
KODOISH, KODOISH, KODOISH, ADONAI 'TSEBAYOTH.
KODOISH, KODOISH, KODOISH, ADONAI 'TSEBAYOTH.

We are going to work with you for a few moments energetically. We are going to realign certain patterns of energy. We are s-t-r-e-t-c-h-i-n-g you energetically to give you a greater capacity for love, for joy, for light. Use this expanded capacity to take in and to funnel through this light and this love to those in your life for whom you feel so deeply.

We would speak to you now about the ascension process which is underway. There are those who see ascension as a blinking out and there are those who see it in other ways. It is simply an increase in frequency, a vibrational upgrade if you will. It can happen instantly or over a period of time. It can happen slowly, little by little, or it can happen rapidly, in the twinkling of an eye.

Frequencies are registered according to the ability of the entity. Let us use the dog whistle analogy. When you blow a dog whistle the vibrational rate is beyond human hearing, but the dog hears and responds. You are surrounded continually by frequencies that you cannot perceive with your five senses. Those around you in the etheric are beyond the vibrational rate of your current ability to see or hear physically and yet they are there.   It is possible to blink out, to increase in vibrational rate even within the physical to where you are invisible. There is validity to the concept of ascension through blinking out.

At this present time there are no plans for a mass blinking out.   There are people who have learned through many many years of discipline to master the process of consciously increasingly their frequency to what you would call ascension. This is based on hard work and diligent study. It is the result of dedicated personal effort, with the use of esoteric knowledge. At the other end of the understanding of this process is the concept held somewhat primitively by some of your orthodox Christians that there shall be a mass gathering up into the clouds of the chosen ones. This is a false concept.

The ascension   now underway is   a co-creative process. There are energies in the higher realms, the angelic realm of the Universal Divine Light Council,

who are working with those who are ready in consciousness to increase their frequency. And these
ones shall master the ability of blinking out and
blinking in. They will not leave this planet perma-
nently, but will have the ability of coming and going
visually to other people.

Does this sound over the edge? It is on the hori-
zon and not far away. There are those who will experience this and it is a co-creative process. People will
not be taken. This will not be the result of some kind
of mass gathering up nor will it be a process totally
dependent upon personal effort. It will be a co-creative process in which each individual who has come
into a consciousness and a resonance with this will
be calibrated - this is the co-creative part - will be calibrated to the extent that it is allowed.

You are moving in this direction. There will come
a time when you will become invisible. You won't
blink out on your loved ones and family, but you
will come into resonance with the I AM Presence to
the extent that there will be a blending. People will
not see you, but rather the I AM that you are.

We are complete.

DAY THIRTEEN

**KODOISH, KODOISH, KODOISH, ADONAI 'TSEBAYOTH.
KODOISH, KODOISH, KODOISH, ADONAI 'TSEBAYOTH.
KODOISH, KODOISH, KODOISH, ADONAI 'TSEBAYOTH.**

We come to you this morning on the wings of the dawn, filling your life with grace. We come to you on the first rays of the sun and with the singing of the birds. We come to you on the clouds that drift across the mountain top and in the whispering of your own heart. We are here. We are always here in myriad ways. All you have to do is listen. We come to you in the stillness of your own spirit, we the emissary.

We have guided you upon the pathway, step by step. If you were to review your life you would see how all choices have been the result of the guidance that we have carefully given to bring you to this point. We have brought you to this point in spite of your doubts, your fears, and the limitations of your consciousness.

You are at a point of transition. You are more conscious of your doubts, but they are fading. We are in the process of fully integrating and aligning ourself with the I AM of your own being. If you will look, you can see most clearly how everything is falling into place. How everything is being arranged.

You have asked for guidance, and we say to you that you have already received this. You are only asking for some kind of solid verbal confirmation. We have given you the guidance in your heart.

Call forth the presence of love which is the divine plan, which is the Holy Spirit, which is the emanation of Divine Presence. Allow that love to permeate every aspect of your being.

This is all. This is enough. We go.

Day Fourteen

KODOISH, KODOISH, KODOISH, ADONAI 'TSEBAYOTH.
KODOISH, KODOISH, KODOISH, ADONAI 'TSEBAYOTH.
KODOISH, KODOISH, KODOISH, ADONAI 'TSEBAYOTH.

There are times when it is difficult for us to integrate into your vibration. This is due to a number of factors, some of which you are aware and some you are not. We can offer several recommendations to help increase the rate of your vibration and to facilitate our integration and communication.

It is a challenge for you, especially as you travel, to maintain certain dietary practices. However we would suggest refraining from eating solid food in the evening. This allows your body to be totally at rest at night when you sleep. Allowing your body to be totally at rest protects you from interference from the astral plane during your sleep. It allows you to be totally restored in body, mind and spirit during your sleep. It allows your vibrations to be tuned to the optimum level so that we are able to integrate easily when you awake and therefore to communicate with you more clearly.

This is the reason it is easier to meditate and communicate with us early in the morning. Not only are the vibrations different early in the morning but, when well rested, you are restored to your natural state which you are able to maintain early in the day. The time will come when you will be able to maintain this vibration throughout the day but, presently, you are doing well to maintain it for a short time when you awaken ... especially when you awaken after a complete rest.

We would recommend that you observe this practice as often as possible. We realize that you have certain social commitments which require you to eat in the evening. We do not ask you to be so rigid in following these practices that you make yourself and others uncomfortable. We are simply saying that, if you observe these practices, you will facilitate the complete rest of your body and the subsequent improved communication with us. We also suggest that you avoid the combination of foods as much as possible. When you eat very very simply, it is less strain on your physical body.

At this time we ask you to go into resonance. Bring yourself into resonance with the essence of the I AM which is love. Allow that to permeate every aspect of your being including your will and your intent. And it shall be thus. We go.

Day Fifteen

KODOISH, KODOISH, KODOISH, ADONAI'TSEBAYOTH.
KODOISH, KODOISH, KODOISH, ADONAI' TSEBAYOTH.
KODOISH, KODOISH, KODOISH, ADONAI 'TSEBAYOTH.

We are here. We come on the rays of the rising sun. We come on the rays of joy. We come on the rays of delight. We come, the emissary of the I AM That I AM, the I AM council. We come to you and through you to reflect with you for a moment. We speak of your personal journey from tragic to magic; from the density of the dream state into the lightness of ascension.

Picture, if you will, being in the depths of the sea in which there are innumerable layers. The lowest depths of the sea are cold and sunless, and the pressure is very intense. As you begin to rise level by level, the pressure become less and the light increases. As you break the surface, you experience the warm tropical sea and the radiant sun. So it is in your own life as you journey from the microcosm to the macrocosm.

We offer another analogy. It is that of the dream

state, or more specifically the nightmare. What you would normally call the dream state sometimes gives rise to this phenomenon, the nightmare. It is a time when you experience intense emotions of fear. If you work with your dream state regularly, you can reach a point of awareness or lucidity within the dream and realize that you are dreaming. Once this is accomplished, you can manipulate its outcome. You can take your nightmare and give it a beautiful ending. It takes practice, and it can be done but, first, you must become aware that you are dreaming.

As you move upward through these intense layers of your dream drama, you will see increasing light. When you finally emerge from this ocean into the light, you will be fully awake.

Do not deceive yourself into thinking that this will happen at the moment of your passing out of this physical body for, wherever you are vibrationally at the moment of your passing, you will continue. You do not awaken at so-called death. You only move into another level of creating your reality or your dream state without the physical equipment.

In one sense, you are on a journey. It is the journey from the microcosm to the macrocosm. It is the journey from fear to love. It is the journey from separation to reunification. It is the journey from he, she, it, them and us to I AM; I AM that I AM.

You have been imprisoned by the bars of fear. Perhaps you have convinced yourself that it is protective custody because it is even more fearful outside your cell.

"What if I stepped out of this prison that I have lived in for eons, for lifetimes? It may be my prison but it is all I have known. It may be my prison, but I know every inch of it. I know every little emotion, however painful. I know every little thought. I know every little quirk. And it's safe here. Yes, sometimes I feel constricted, but it is safe. What if? What if I took the key that I have possessed all along, opened the door, stepped out of this prison, and realized that it was of my own making; realized that I was not only the prisoner but the warden as well. What if I realized that outside of these bars was the possibility of fully coming into the awakened state of love; fully coming into the acknowledgment of the who I AM; fully coming into the truth."

Know this: The truth of who you are and for what you are destined as a species - that truth will make you free.

We invite you into silence now that we may work

with you energetically to bring about a shifting, an opening .... a movement of this prison door .... to set it ajar. We can open it, but only you can walk outside. That may be only sticking a toe out and quickly pulling it back because it feels safer inside. It might be sticking a foot out. It might be stepping outside, becoming fear-filled, and going back inside for a few more lifetimes. Or it might be throwing the door wide open, stepping outside and saying "Here am I, Oh Lord, take me."

As the flowers in Spring, we each bloom according to our own schedule. So, let us be in a place of resonance for a moment with you to the extent of your own timing, to the extent of your own allowing. Allow this shifting, this work to take place within you.

We invoke the presence of Divine Grace that it might come into your life; that it might enfold you with a blanket of protection, with a blanket of beauty, with a blanket of harmony, with a blanket of love. We invoke Divine Grace that you might come into resonance with your own soul, with your own spirit, with Divine Presence, with the I AM of who you are.

We are complete.

Day Sixteen

KODOISH, KODOISH, KODOISH, ADONAI'TSEBAYOTH.
KODOISH, KODOISH, KODOISH, ADONAI'TSEBAYOTH.
KODOISH, KODOISH, KODOISH, ADONAI'TSEBAYOTH.

What is it we can say that you do not already know at the depth of your being? What is it that we can do except to call you out of that minute corner of consciousness where you dwell and into the fullness of the I AM presence. What can we say? This only: Step out into Spring. Leave the coldness, the Winter of your prison. Leave it behind. Step out of your dream-prison. Awaken into the fullness, into the light, into the beauty of the I AM that you are.

So it is, we come this morning simply to commune. Let us be present together in unity. Let us allow our energies to blend. Let us reunite into the knowing of who and what we are. Let us experience the mystical union of remembering the I AM that I AM.

We have spoken of the increasing frequency of your vibrations as you move more fully into love.

You may have wondered, "How is this to be?" It will come as a result of your own effort and practice. There is fear and there is love. Moment by moment, you choose between the two. There is judgment and there is love. Moment by moment you choose between the two.

Each morning and each evening as you sit in reflection, look at each person in your life for whom you hold judgment or blame of any kind. Focus on that person, situation or behavior which is the source of your judgment. Now, accept the possibility that this situation, this experience, this manner of being is purposeful in his or her life. It may be purposeful in ways that you do not discern. Step out of your micro-cosmic lilliputian perspective and see as we see .... from the big picture .... and know that it is all perfect. Do not allow your pain or anger to lead you into the false role of judge, jury and executioner. Know that you are the lover and all is in Divine Order. Enfold in love that person with all those personality traits and behaviors that you abhor. Enfold in love all of the unpleasant experiences you have had with that person. They are in Divine Order. They are perfect. From the big picture of the I AM presence, enfold that person in love. As you do this, your own frequency increases .... increases and increases .... and miracles happen.

You will be unable to accomplish this fully until you have looked deep within yourself and have identified those points of judgment and blame of yourself. Are there aspects of yourself that you judge and blame? These are simply your instructors. They are part of the dream drama of your curriculum. Enfold them in love. Enfold them in acceptance, and then release them.

It is your attachment to blame and judgment of self that truly imprisons you. You were not "born in sin." You were born in innocence and, at your core, that is who you are even now. As you accept this and allow the all-pervading love of the I AM to enfold you, your eyes will be opened to your true nature. You will come to understand the importance of these experiences, these aspects of yourself, and the very act of acknowledgement and acceptance releases and dissolves them. As this happens your frequency increases. You may ask, "Is it possible to release all blame? Is it possible to release all judgment? Is it possible to release all of this about myself and about others? Is it possible to become one in mind and heart with the I AM that I AM that I AM?"

We say to you in all gravity that, as you move into the new vibration in this next phase of the evolution of your planet, it is not only possible, it is absolutely essential. We are giving you survival skills, so to speak.

You do not need to learn how to rub sticks together to create a fire. You do not need to learn how to dig roots and find berries for your survival. You need only to learn how to increase the frequency of the essence of your being and to integrate into the essence of the I AM that I AM that you are - the I AM which is love.

In the times which are coming, there is only one place which is safe. It is not this vortex or that mountain top. It is not some far-away island or cave. It is not an ET mothership. It is your heart in which there dwells no fear. It is your heart in which there dwells no judgment. It is your heart in which there dwells no blame. It is your heart which is filled and which radiates the love of the I AM that I AM that I AM.

Your work is cut out for you. It is not some great mission of saving the world, though there is work to be done there. No, it is within your own heart. The work is within your own spirit. The work is within your own remembering who you are, why you are here, and what this is all about. The work is accomplished as the global thought-forms of fear, judgment, blame and hatred dissolve. It is accomplished each time one truly awakens from the dream drama of this nightmare.

So, we leave you in peace. We leave you in light. We leave you in beauty. We are the emissary of the I AM that I AM. We go saying with all the host of Heaven, Kodoish, Kodoish, Kodoish, Adonai 'Tsebayoth. Kodoish, Kodoish, Kodoish, Adonai 'Tsebayoth. Kodoish, Kodoish, Kodoish, Adonai 'Tsebayoth. We go.

DAY SEVENTEEN

KODOISH, KODOISH, KODOISH, ADONAI' TSEBAYOTH.
KODOISH, KODOISH, KODOISH, ADONAI 'TSEBAYOTH.
KODOISH, KODOISH, KODOISH, ADONAI 'TSEBAYOTH.

We come to you now from the place beyond words, beyond thoughts. We come from the heart of the Christos, from the place of pure love. We are the emissary, the emanations of the I AM that I AM. We come to take your hand and lead you into the land of delight. We come to awaken you from your long slumber, from your dark dream. We come to bring you again into the garden which is Eden; the garden of your own spirit, the garden of remembering who you are; the garden of love.

Each morning, you bow in homage to El Shadai, the God who is more than enough. So, we carry you beyond the realm of words, beyond the realm of thoughts and into the realm of pure being. We carry you into the realm of pure delight, into the realm of pure joy, into the realm of pure love. As you contemplate the wonders of El Shadai, the wonders of Adonai, you are transformed in the twinkling of an eye.

We come as an emissary of the Most High in response to your prayers. For indeed, you could not listen to the voice of God without being utterly and wholly overwhelmed. So, from the Presence of the Most High we come to answer you.

Your prayers were known even before they were uttered, even before they were formed in your thoughts. Your needs are known to the Most High. Not only have your needs been known, but your needs are already being met even now. There is a timing for everything. Seeds have been planted. Seeds have germinated. Seeds have taken root and seeds are growing. It is the time of the fulfillment, the time of growing. You will, very soon see these growing plants and they will come into harvest. The prayers that you have uttered have already been answered. It is only a small matter of timing for their manifestation, and all of this is given to you in love.

It is complete. We go.

Day Eighteen

**KODOISH, KODOISH, KODOISH, ADONAI TSEBAYOTH.
KODOISH, KODOISH, KODOISH, ADONAI TSEBAYOTH.
KODOISH, KODOISH, KODOISH, ADONAI TSEBAYOTH.**

We are here. We are here in the full presence, in the full glory, and in the full power of the I AM presence, the I AM that I AM. From the place beyond words, from the place beyond thought, from the place beyond concept, we touch into the tininess of your reality. We cross the great abyss of your understanding .... the fathomless abyss .... with a minute fraction of energy that is a hologram of the I AM. We are the emissary of The Unutterable. We are the emissary of The Incomprehensible; El Shadai, Adonai, Allah, Wakan Tanka, Great Mystery, I AM that I AM.

We are s-t-r-e-c-h-i-n-g the very limits of whom you are physically, mentally; calibrating .... to bring you more than you bargained for. We offer you a hot tub of bliss. Even as your inspiration has often come to you in the shower, so do we now invite you to soak in your hot tub of bliss a bit each day. It will warm your heart. It will heal your body. It will allow you to fly on the magic carpet of love.

We are complete.

DAY NINETEEN

KODOISH, KODOISH, KODOISH, ADONAI 'TSEBAYOTH.
KODOISH, KODOISH, KODOISH, ADONAI 'TSEBAYOTH.
KODOISH, KODOISH, KODOISH, ADONAI 'TSEBAYOTH.

We come to you in the radiance of the presence of the I AM that I AM. We come to you from across the fathomless abyss of understanding, touching into that tiny corner of your illusion which you call reality. Yes, we are here, closer than the beating of your own heart and, in other ways, further than the outer edges of infinity.

We come to you this morning to speak of the Divine Presence, that which you call God. We come to you in light, and we come to you lightly.

We see, at times, a certain heaviness in you. Have you noticed the deeper you sink into the illusion of your mind-drama the heavier you become? To use an example, the deeper you go into the sea, the less light and more pressure there is. The closer you come to the surface, the more light there is and the lighter you become. So this morning, we are gently bringing you closer to the surface, to that point where reality and illusion meet. From this point, we would speak to you about God in drag.

This may bring an amusing image to your mind. God in drag. And what is drag? It is one thing dressed up like or pretending to be something else. When you see someone performing in drag, does it not bring a smile to your face? This is true not only because of the pretense involved, but also because there is often an exaggeration of that which is being imitated. So, you see the man in drag acting out a feminine role that is more stereotypically feminine than you would actually see in a biological woman. That is a part of the comedy of it all.

We suggest to you this morning that your life, your world, your "reality" is filled every moment of every day with God in drag.

We would invite you now to shift your perspective and begin to see God in drag. A drag show brings a big smile to your face and lots of laughs. In truth it en-lightens you. However, you take quite seriously this drama with which you are involved day by day. You believe that the green pieces of paper in your purse are something other than green pieces of paper with photos of dead men. How amusing! Don't you see? It is God in drag.

The person that confronts you, that criticizes you, that condemns you, that blames you, that takes advantage of you, this person that brings up all of your stuff. Who is it? God in drag. And who is this one, whom in your mythology you call the evil one, Satan? Who is he but God in drag. For indeed, there is nothing within the context of the mind drama of your dream that is not God in drag, the One appearing as the many.

All of the actors on the stage of your personal drama and the dramas of your species, all of them are God in drag. They perform to en-lighten you; to bring you to the light of the awareness of who you are.

When a man dresses as a woman and goes on stage, playing the role and responding to the laughter, applause, and encouragement of the audience, in his own mind, he can indeed become that woman. In the midst of the drama and with the consensus of the audience, he forgets that his biology is male.

So it is with your species. As you become deeply involved in your own drama, you go into a deep state of amnesia and begin to believe that the role that you are playing is who you really are. You soon forget that all the actors upon your stage including yourself, are God in drag.

This is simply another way of presenting to you and having you reflect upon and contemplate that which we have been saying again and again and again. Everything that you are experiencing in this third dimensional drama is just that; it is drama. You have been so thoroughly captivated by the props and the plot that you don't even realize the extent of your amnesia.

When we have sent prophetic voices in the past, what has happened to them? Humanity has risen up and said, "We do not want to awaken from this dream, leave us alone." Over and over and over again, we have endeavored to awaken you from the dark dream, from the amnesia of your true identity. You can awaken in one of two ways. It can be done with a gentle kiss, a magical kiss, a kiss of love. Or, if you are a hard sleeper, we can simply turn the bed upside down. You can experience a rude awakening instead of a gentle awakening. The choice is yours.

Now, this is what we are asking of you. We are asking you to become fully awake. Awaken to who you are. As you truly open your eyes, you will see God in drag in all aspects of your life. Become the lover. Cultivate the frequency of love in your life and become the blue prince, the beautiful princess to whom we may bestow the magical kiss of awakening.

We have spoken to you repeatedly of love. Perhaps it has sounded like soupy spiritual platitudes. No, we are talking about the most powerful, the most searing, the most transformative energy that exists in the universe. We are endeavoring to work with you, to clarify, purify and increase this frequency which will allow its power to totally dominate your life with clarity. Have you wondered why? It is because we are calling you, asking you, inviting you to become a prince - a prince who will bestow the magic kiss of love that will break the spell of enchantment and awaken the sleeping beauty of your true nature, the I AM that I AM.

Why are we choosing you? It is not a thing of the ego for that is simply a part of the drama. You are not the only prince or princess. There are scores awakening this moment to their royal nature. We are working with you and through you because you have expressed honestly and sincerely at a heart level to totally surrender to the I AM presence and to the Divine Will. You are not particularly good at surrendering. We see that. You have control issues. Sometimes you're obstinate and stubborn, but we know the sincerity of your heart and we are able to work with that. It is laborious sometimes, but we see you as you can be, not as you are. We see in you God in drag.

So, we invite you moment by moment to go into deeper levels of surrender, to deeper levels of trust. Each morning, to the extent that you truly surrender to the Divine Will, it will not be necessary for you to have those experiences in your life which will test that surrendered state. We say to you, practice, practice, practice. Every decision, go within, surrender and say, "What should I do?" The more you practice, the clearer the communication, understanding and guidance.

We say finally that, every action and every thought directed toward another person .... whether of good or bad intent, whether of praise or of blame, whether of acceptance or of judgment .... is an action and a thought directed toward God - God in drag.

In the power, in the glory, in the light of the I AM that I AM, we came and we go, saying continually with all the hosts of Heaven, Kodoish, Kodoish, Kodoish, Adonai Tsebayoth. Kodoish, Kodoish, Kodoish, Adonai 'Tsebayoth. Kodoish, Kodoish, Kodoish, Adonai 'Tsebayoth.

DAY TWENTY

KODOISH, KODOISH, KODOISH, ADONAI 'TSEBAYOTH.
KODOISH, KODOISH, KODOISH, ADONAI 'TSEBAYOTH.
KODOISH, KODOISH, KODOISH, ADONAI 'TSEBAYOTH.

We come to you this morning joyfully in the full presence of the Most High I AM that I AM. We come this morning into the very core of your being. We come into the temple of your heart, touching your spirit in joy, in peace and in love.

Moment by moment, practice the Presence of God, the Great Mystery, El Shadai, Adonai, Allah, Wakan Tanka, The Christos. Step out of your drama. Awaken from your dream. Come into remembrance of who you really are and move deeper and deeper into communion with the I AM that I AM that you are.

As you do this, love will gradually replace all judgment. Lightness will replace all darkness. Truth will replace all ignorance. Unity will replace all separation. Your spirit will be refined. Your heart will be opened. Your frequency will increase exponentially, and you will be in a state of love continually.

We have planted the seed. We have created the conditions for its growth. We have brought it to the point of germination. The angelic ones will be with you continually, nurturing and nourishing the seedling that you are. They will protect and guide you with Divine Light that you may come into the full maturity, remembrance, strength and power of who you are as a manifestation of the I AM that I AM.

At all times, allow yourself to be rooted in the soil and stability of the Most High from whence you derive your nourishment. Allow your heart and your spirit to open to the spring sunshine of the Most High from whence you derive your nourishment. Continually surrender everything which is not in alignment with the Divine. As you do, you will fulfill that for which you came. You came, not for some great mission, nor fame, nor fortune, but simply *to be in love.*

Surrender every challenge, every decision, every situation, and every choice to the designs of love which is the Divine Plan of the I AM that I AM that you are. Practice the Divine Presence of the I AM that I AM and surrender all in love.

With the whole hosts of Heaven, the angels, the archangels, the cherubim, the seraphim, with all the hosts, we say and sing continuously, Kodoish, Kodoish, Kodoish, Adonai 'Tsebayoth. Kodoish, Kodoish, Kodoish, Adonai 'Tsebeyoth. Kodoish, Kodoish, Kodoish, Adonai 'Tsebeyoth. We go.

DAY TWENTY ONE

KODOISH, KODOISH, KODOISH, ADONAI TSEBAYOTH.
KODOISH, KODOISH, KODOISH, ADONAI TSEBAYOTH.
KODOISH, KODOISH, KODOISH, ADONAI TSEBAYOTH.

We have come into resonance with you again this morning to give you an image. Imagine if you will the image of a child going to bed on Christmas Eve knowing that, during the night, Santa Claus will come and when she awakens there will be gifts and goodies under the Christmas Tree.

She goes to bed with this beautiful thought and a smile on her face and drops into a deep sleep. Then the dreams come to this little one, perhaps even a nightmare. There is all of this drama going on in the mind, and she thrashes in her bed, crying out in fear or pain. Then, at the right moment, she awakens and remembers it is Christmas morning, and everything changes. Suddenly, there is the remembrance. She looks under the tree and there are all these wonderful gifts.

So, we are saying to you that the nightmare is over. How will you awaken? Will it be a magic kiss or are you too deeply asleep? How long will it take you to realize that the nightmare is over and it is Christmas morning?

We have placed a gift under your tree. It is a magic wand with which you can touch anything and it will be transformed. What is this magic? It is that magical perspective that allows you to let go of judgment and of seeing the I AM that I AM in everything around you. There are those who awaken from the nightmare only long enough to yawn, not remembering that it is Christmas, and drift again into the dream.

So you see, it is not a matter of changing your circumstances. Is not the big basket of gifts under the tree even as you are lying there in the throes of the nightmare? Is it not all there now? It is only a matter of awakening and remembering. The real magic is simply a shift in your perspective. When you make this shift, you realize that everything around you, even your nightmare and all those scary characters chasing you, are just God in drag - there to help you awaken.

What are we saying to you that we have not said already? Nothing. But sometimes you need more prodding, more reminding.

And so it is, we go.

Day Twenty Two

KODOISH, KODOISH, KODOISH, ADONAI 'TSEBAYOTH.
KODOISH, KODOISH, KODOISH, ADONAI 'TSEBAYOTH.
KODOISH, KODOISH, KODOISH, ADONAI 'TSEBAYOTH.

We come to you now, we come through you, we come in spite of you. We touch into your heart. We touch into that part which is connected. We touch into that part of you that remembers; that part of you which knows. We call you to that place within yourself that remembers.

We speak to you this morning of the Lenten season; these 40 days that are observed in honor of the time spent by the Master Jesus fasting in the desert. We would say to you that, contrary to that which is normally taught by the priests and the dogma of your religion, this is not a time of sacrifice. The I AM that I AM that you are does not require sacrifice; does not require blood or pain.

The true meaning of this season is that of clarification. When the Master Jesus, the reflection so pure of the I AM that I AM, went into the desert, it was a time to set aside all of those things which were pulling him this way and that. As you step aside from the physical demands of life, you are freer to move into the inner sanctum of your own spirit and commune with that of yourself which is of the I AM that I AM.

So, this time that is observed as Lent is not for the purpose of sacrifice but for the purpose of simplification. At this time, it is a custom to release certain things. In the past, perhaps, you did this in the spirit of sacrifice or simply in the observance of the season but, in truth, look at what is in fact taking place. By stepping away for a moment or two from the intensity of this curriculum which you have chosen, you have had an opportunity to move more clearly into an inner space and view your life from a different perspective.

Now, we speak metaphorically. Each of you has chosen a certain curriculum. All of your experiences are a part of this curriculum. Your relationships - curriculum. Your financial concerns - curriculum. Your health concerns - curriculum. Everything that you have ever experienced, however joyous or painful, has been a part of your curriculum. You can look at it in retrospect and see how you have expanded, learned and grown from this curriculum.

So, this period of 40 days is not a time of sacrifice.

It is like spring break. It is a time to get away from the demands of your curriculum. It is a time to relax a bit from the heaviness and intensity of anything of a physical nature which keeps you locked into the dream drama. It is a time to disengage and see your world from a broader perspective.

Let us speak with another metaphor, the professional student. This is one who goes to the university and becomes so enthralled with college life that he prolongs the experience far beyond that which is usual or ordinary. This can also take place spiritually. In fact, it takes place spiritually with most people. They may be devoted to their religions and do those things they are told to do by their priests and ministers but, often, they fail to grow spiritually and never graduate into the realms of deeper understanding of the I AM that I AM that they are. They are professional students. They move in a circle instead of a spiral. It is as if there were a glass ceiling.

At the end of this period of reflection, as you celebrate the time of the resurrection of love, you will make a choice whether to return to those things that you released during this time. We say to you that there is no right or wrong in these matters. Yet there are consequences. Everything has consequences. If you go this way, there will be these consequences. If you go that way, there will be other consequences. Ultimately it will simply be a part of your curriculum as you grow and expand from lifetime to lifetime.

We give you a gift during this season of reflection. It is the gift of Love. There is only one thing that is truly of value and importance. The true religion - regardless of the name - is not a matter of holy books, dogma, rituals, robes or religious paraphernalia. It is that place in your heart where you come to awaken and to remember your connection to the I AM that I AM. It is that place of original innocence within yourself which is beyond all judgment and all blame of yourself or others. It is love.

The poets, musicians and artists each attempt to speak of it, but we say to you that love is simply that deep connection that is without judgment. It must be first and foremost love for yourself. Because of the nature of your origin - part God and part animal - you are indeed in judgment of yourself. You see all the things you might have done differently. You see all of the things that perhaps you should have done and you feel that you didn't. And there is judgment.

When you were a child and studying a subject that was very difficult, perhaps one such as mathematics, part of the learning and problem-solving involved making mistakes in calculation. When you made these mistakes, did you beat your chest and say, "How evil am I, how wrong am I?" Probably not. You realized that your mistakes were only a lack of understanding of how it works. Your mistakes were not from evil intent but from miscalculation. That which you have or have not done in the past and for which you hold judgment is simply the result of your microcosmic perspective. In the tiny corner of your consciousness, in your dream drama, you cannot possibly understand the true nature of reality. So you miscalculate and make mistakes which bring you pain.

Do you fear that you will hurt others? Truly you cannot. Others choose their pain individually or collectively as a result of how they choose to view the experiences in their lives. They choose to be hurt or to be delighted or to be whatever as a result of your actions.

Even those actions which are designed to hurt are born of ignorance. Revenge, for example, is a natural response to your own hurt, but only so within the microcosm or dream drama. When you awaken into the macrocosm and begin to see God in drag, you realize that revenge toward another is revenge toward

God. You cannot strike out at God, the I AM that I AM that you are, without injuring yourself. Revenge, simply put, is dumb. It is like shooting yourself in the foot. You are diminished.

Why do we devote so much time speaking of judgment, blame, fear, innocence and love? Because it is here, in your heart, that the flame of the great I AM that I AM that you are is lit and kept burning. If you are able to maintain that flame moment by moment, day by day, it will illuminate your entire life, and your life in turn will illuminate the world.

We embrace you in the total acceptance of the I AM that I AM that you are as a manifestation of love. All of the doctrines and all of the teachings, all of the great chants and all of the religious robes; all of it of all religions does not equal an ounce of love from the Source of that which is beyond thought, beyond concept, that which we only truly know in love.

Your vibrational frequency now is about to be upgraded. Look deep into the eyes of those around you, and you will see God in drag. That person in your life who challenges you; who is he but God in drag. He is the One appearing as the many. And so you yourself, as an aspect of the I AM that I AM, are God in drag. As you look deep into the eyes of each person in your life, those you embrace and those you avoid, you will see God.

We go now, saying and singing with the whole host of Heaven, Kodoish, Kodoish, Kodoish, Adonai 'Tsebayoth. Kodoish, Kodoish, Kodoish, Adonai 'Tsebayoth. Kodoish, Kodoish, Kodoish, Adonai 'Tsebayoth.

DAY TWENTY THREE

KODOISH, KODOISH, KODOISH, ADONAI 'TSEBAYOTH.
KODOISH, KODOISH, KODOISH, ADONAI 'TSEBAYOTH.
KODOISH, KODOISH, KODOISH, ADONAI' TSEBAYOTH.

It is with joy that we return. There is a joy in our coming together once again. If you look about you, you will see that you are in fact an alchemist. You are learning how to take base metals, so to speak, and transform them into gold.

You are in a time of great cultural turbulence and upheaval. There is a scurrying about, looking this way and that, searching for something solid to hold onto. Some attempt to anchor themselves in human religion that is absolute, pretending to have all of the answers. Some anchor themselves into materialism which seems solid. Others anchor themselves in to various forms of the physical.

We are of the heart. We stand as a bridge between the higher realms and higher dimensions and the physical realms. The teachings we bring to you are those of balance, of being centered in the heart and filtering all that you would look at through the heart.

So we are of the heart. Our teachings are of the heart.

Within your heart is a vast universe of possibilities; possibilities born of love, possibilities born of innocence, possibilities born of purity. We invite you out of the basement of your physicality, out of the attic of your mentality, out of the basement of your emotionality, out of the attic of your spirituality and into the chambers of your heart, the chambers of wisdom, the chambers of integration and the chambers of balance.

You are a holographic unit of the I AM that I AM. You are god but not God. You are not pure spirit. You are physical. You are material. You are sexual. Yet, you are also more than these. We invite you to bring all of these aspects into your own heart as the place of integration, the workshop, the cauldron of the alchemist.

As you bring these higher and lower energies together into the cauldron of your heart, there is created an absolutely transformative magic which will produce gold. That gold, that magic elixir, that rosetta stone is love. Love your body. Love your physicality. Love your sexuality. Love your mentality. Love your spirituality. Bring them all together in the center of your heart and allow them to bloom into the energy of love that extends out to all people everywhere, to all situations everywhere. Become a light-house of love and radiate the light of your love to all people, to all situations. As you do, you are automatically connected with your Source, that which you call God.

We are complete.

DAY TWENTY FOUR

KODOISH, KODOISH, KODOISH, ADONAI 'TSEBAYOTH.
KODOISH, KODOISH, KODOISH, ADONAI 'TSEBAYOTH.
KODOISH, KODOISH, KODOISH, ADONAI' TSEBAYOTH.

We come to you in resonance, in joy and in love, overshadowing you this beautiful morning as you await the rising of the sun. We touch in to assist you in increasing your vibrational frequency to one of greater joy. Let this be a day of light. Let this be a day of joy. Let this be a day of rejoicing.

We fill your heart with the light of the Presence and this light flows through you and integrates with you at a cellular level so that you are a being of pure joy, of pure light and of Divine Grace.

Because we function from the macrocosm, we see things so differently than you do from the microcosm, the little picture. Because we are able to resonate with your thoughts, we are able to tune in, see the world from your perspective, and hold it in the light of our macrocosmic perspective of the big picture. Sometimes we are amused by the difference.

However, it does give us a greater understanding of your little anxieties, of your little desires and yes, of your lack of faith. Now, because we see the big picture, we see what was, what is and what shall be. At least, this is the way you perceive it in your time-bound dimension. From our macrocosmic perspective, we can say to you, reiterate with total assurance, that all is well. Because you are in a time-bound dimension, you see your good ahead of you. But we say to you, it is already here. To the extent that you can fully acknowledge and accept this, you will experience it.

We enfold you now with the love of creation, the love of the I AM that I AM that you are. Bring yourself into resonance with the rising sun. Let your voice blend with the angelic ones in praising the Most High, El Shadai, the God who is more than enough.

So we are complete.

Day Twenty Five

KODOISH, KODOISH, KODOISH, ADONAI 'TSEBAYOTH.
KODOISH, KODOISH, KODOISH, ADONAI 'TSEBAYOTH.
KODOISH, KODOISH, KODOISH, ADONAI' TSEBAYOTH.

We come to you today on the wings of the dawn, holding you in the presence of the Most High, the I AM that I AM that you are. We, your angels and archangels, cherubim and seraphim bear you now before the throne of The Most Holy One. In the radiance of that Presence you are filled, you are immersed in light, Divine Radiance, in love, love in which no shadows exist.

We come lightly, nudging you to lighten up on yourself and those you love. If you could see from our perspective of the macrocosm you would see what a tiny, tiny, tiny part of that which you call you is actually connected into this third-dimensional drama that you call reality. It is barely 1%. The heaviness you experience is all within that tiny fraction immersed in the dream. Are you aware of the other 99%?

We command for you that this be a day of Grace. May you move through the day permeated and filled with Grace. May Divine Love, Divine Grace, Divine Creative Energies enfold and radiate from you. Allow your heart to be as the sun. Allow it to shine forth the energy of the Most High; without impediment, without clouds, without judgment.

Let the warm rays of your own heart touch each person in your life today. We blend with you now. This day we bring about a blending so that we become one with you. We bring you to Eden and nourish you with the manna of Divine Presence.

If you could understand from our perspective, from the macrocosm, you would see such a tiny, tiny part of that which you call you actually connected into this third-dimensional drama that you call reality. If you could see as we see, you would understand you are 99.99% of the cosmic, then your consciousness would shift.

Your primary work is that of increasing the frequency of love and extending that out from yourself. We go.

DAY TWENTY SIX

KODOISH, KODOISH, KODOISH, ADONAI 'TSEBAYOTH.
KODOISH, KODOISH, KODOISH, ADONAI 'TSEBAYOTH.
KODOISH, KODOISH, KODOISH, ADONAI' TSEBAYOTH.

W e are the emissary of the Universal Divine Light Council and we come to you today with great joy, with great love and with great light, and we come to you lightly. We come to you from the inner regions of your own heart, and we come to you from beyond the edge of infinity. We come to you in truth and in resonance.

You are about to experience a profound shift. There is the story, as you know, of the little boy who cried wolf. He did this so many times that people ceased to listen to him. So, there is a part of you that has heard so many times of this pending shift that you are in deep doubt for there have been wise ones who have said "It is now." and it didn't happen. "It is now." and, again, "It is upon us." and it did not happen, so you are in great doubt.

We say to you that this pending shift is of an inner, as well as of an outer nature. It has been your knowing for some time that there will not be the kind of devastating polar shift that some have suggested and that some have foreseen. But there will be and, in fact, there is in progress at this moment, a profound shift in consciousness. Throughout the world, there will be trouble and tribulation. There has always been trouble and tribulation throughout the world. There will be a certain increase in this among those people who remain asleep, locked into the dream drama of consensus reality.

It is difficult for you to see how this tremendous shift will take place. Your media continues to focus on the nightmare, and it is hard for you to see. But we say to you that it is like an iceberg. That which is visible on top is the darkness; evil if you will. That which is below the surface is growing, building, and gathering mass, and this is the new consciousness. There will come a time, and that time is not far off, when this iceberg will flip and, suddenly, that which seemed so dominant will be dissolved by the light of the sun and will be submerged. That which was not so visible will come to the fore. This is the great awakening. We compare it with the surprise you experienced at the sudden collapse of the Berlin Wall.

What is your work during this time of the shifting

of consciousness? It is to channel light. And what is light but love. Continue focusing this light and helping others to focus it to dissolve and melt that which is of darkness.

And so it is, we go.

Day Twenty Seven

KODOISH, KODOISH, KODOISH, ADONAI 'TSEBAYOTH.
KODOISH, KODOISH, KODOISH, ADONAI 'TSEBAYOTH.
KODOISH, KODOISH, KODOISH, ADONAI' TSEBAYOTH.

We come to you again in light, as the rising sun, reconnecting you with the Source of your being. We come filling you with the joy of the Presence of the I AM that I AM that you are. We come to you, we come through you, we hover about you, waiting with you in anticipation of the rising of the sun, the advent of joy.

Indeed you know that joy is ever-present. It is not something in the future. It is ever-present, and it requires only your acknowledgment, your acceptance and your allowance. So we are here in joy, and we see that there is a frequency increase slowly taking place as you cultivate love and joy in your life.

We see a great harmony at work. There is the planting, cultivating and growing of your garden. This is also taking place as you work with yourself physically, mentally, emotionally and spiritually.

You are on the right track. Continue to be consistent.   Continue to work with yourself energetically. For that truly is the only thing you have to offer the world. It is not your struggle for peace.   It is not your struggle for justice. No, the real contribution is you yourself. We speak not only to you but also to any individual who has chosen to manifest at this time in this dimension. The true contribution is the energy of your own presence. The highest calibration of that energy is love, and the fruit and expression of that energy is joy.

So let today be a day of joy. Let today be a day of sunshine. Let today be a day of love. Cultivate love for yourself, all aspects of yourself, free of judgment. Cultivate love for those around you; those you hold dear and those with whom you have issues. Allow the Divine Grace of Omnipotent Presence, the Source of all good, the I AM that I AM, flow through you and bless the world.

So it is in joy, it is in love, it is in light that we enfold you and we bless you. We go.

DAY TWENTY EIGHT

**KODOISH, KODOISH, KODOISH, ADONAI 'TSEBAYOTH.
KODOISH, KODOISH, KODOISH, ADONAI 'TSEBAYOTH.
KODOISH, KODOISH, KODOISH, ADONAI' TSEBAYOTH.**

From the heart of the Christos; from the center-point of The Unutterable, The Incomprehensible, the Allah, we come. We come as an emissary of the Universal Divine Light Council. We come from the center-point of your own heart. We come to you and we come from you as a hologram of the great I AM. We come to you in joy. We come to you in beauty. We come to you as a frequency, downloading and translating into words from a place beyond words. We now make the necessary adjustments to speak to you; to speak to you at a cellular, vibrational level.

We speak to you energetically of that which is beyond your intellectual or mental ability to fathom. And yet we speak to you of that which is of your own nature. And we say to you that the only way to understand that of which we speak is love.

And so this term that we have used with you; this concept we have spoken to you about so many times;

this concept you have heard over and over again is a pathway of understanding. It is not only a pathway of understanding, it is the pathway of understanding the nature of the Divine, the nature of that one you call El Shadai, the Christos, Allah, Wakan, the Great Mystery.

You have heard the term unconditional love many times. The very term is redundant. To say unconditional love is to say wet water. It is to say cold ice. It is to say hot fire. For the nature of ice is cold. The very nature of water is wet. The very nature of fire is hot. And so the very nature of love is that which is without conditions. We invite you to leap from the concept of unconditional love to that of fearless love. Yes, we admit that this term is also redundant. Because where love is there can be no fear. There is no accommodation for fear in the heart that is truly possessed by love

Let us follow this thought for a moment. Most of your religions and much of your understanding of the spiritual is based on the concept of duality; of good and evil, of darkness and light. This is so much so that these have been developed into archetypes. In your own dominant religion, there are the archetypes of good and evil; of Christ and Satan. As you look into most religions you will find that evil has been personified. This of course has created a problem for those who believe in the ultimate power and unity of the Creator, of the I AM that I AM.

How can the great I AM have a rival? Indeed the I AM is the all that is. How can there be a rival? And yet there is this problem of apparent duality to be explained. As you look into your day to day situation, you see what appears to be the struggle between good and evil, between light and darkness. Yes, within the dream state there is an energy of duality. But it is of your own collective

creation, a shadow puppet on the wall. These are not entities. There is no architect of evil. But there are frequencies, demons if you will, born of fear, anger, hatred, greed and all the rest. They exist only to the extent that they are continually fed within your nightmare. When you awake, they disappear. So there is love and there is fear. Both are enthroned in the heart of your species. And so you are of a dual nature, of a dual allegiance, of a dual heart.

Among your ancient people, the Hopi, there is the term "two hearted" which means to be false. That is compared to one hearted which is to be true. We say that your species is two hearted in that you are locked into the illusion of duality. You pay dual allegiance to love and fear. Can there be love when there is fear? We say no. There can be desire. There can be obsession. There can be neediness. There can be lust. There can be all of these things and more but there cannot be love when there is fear. You cannot truly love God, the I AM that I AM when you are also in fear of that One.

So we invite you to look at the points of fear within yourself. Does not fear itself show a lack of trust; a lack of belief in the I AM that I AM that you are? You have heard it said, "fear God". But we say to you, release your fear of God. To say fear God is to say fear love. For if it is truly love, there is no fear. Where God reigns there is no fear.

So we call you into the temple of the Great I AM. We invite you into the temple of love. We invite you into the temple of delight. We invite you into the temple wherein dwells your Source. Come into the temple of light, into the temple of truth, into the temple of reality. Put on the white robes innocence and truth. Come into the temple of love.

Step out of fear. Step out of the world of chaos. Step into the inner sanctum, the Shangri-La of your own spirit. There re-discover your heart, a heart possessed and consumed by love - that energy of connection that knows no fear, that knows no judgement, that knows no blame. And as you come into alignment and resonance with that energy your frequency is speeded up faster and faster and faster. Come into synchronization with love, with the Divine Presence, with a joy and an ecstasy that fills your being and allows you to soar on the magic carpet up beyond the edges of infinity.

By your love the world is transformed. All that you see, all that you hear, all you count as reality; beneath it all there are simply patterns of energy, energy that you create unconsciously. And this can destroy the world or it can transform the world into the Eden which is your birthright. We go.

New Moon Chart

1997

FEB 7th (7 p.m.) in Scorpio
MARCH 9th (1 p.m.) in Pisces
APRIL 7th (11 a.m.) in Aries
MAY 6th (9 p.m.) in Taurus
JUNE 5th (7 a.m.) in Gemini
JULY 4th (7 p.m.) in Cancer
AUG 3rd (8 a.m.) in Leo
SEPT 1st (11:52 a.m.) in Virgo
OCT 1st (5 p.m.) in Libra
OCT 31st (10 a.m.) in Scorpio
NOV 30th (2 a.m.) in Scorpio
DEC 29th (5 p.m.) in Capricorn

1998

JAN 28th (6 a.m.) in Aquarius
FEB 26th (5 p.m.) in Pisces
MARCH 28th (3 a.m.) in Aries
APRIL 26th (11 a.m.) in Taurus
MAY 25th (7 p.m.) in Gemini
JUNE 24th (4 a.m.) in Cancer
JULY 23rd (2 p.m.) in Leo
AUG 22nd (2 a.m.) in Leo
SEPT 20th (5 p.m.) in Virgo
OCT 20th (10 a.m.) in Libra
NOV 19th (4 a.m.) in Scorpio
DEC 18th (11 p.m.) in Sagittarius

1999

JAN 17th (4 p.m.) in Capricorn
FEB 16th (7 a.m.) in Aquarius
MARCH 17th (7 p.m.) in Pisces
APRIL 16th (4 a.m.) in Aries
MAY 15th (noon) in Taurus
JUNE 13th (7 p.m.) in Gemini
JULY 13th (2 a.m.) in Cancer
AUG 11th (11 a.m.) in Leo
SEPT 9th (10 p.m.) in Virgo
OCT 9th (11 a.m.) in Libra
NOV 8th (4 a.m.) in Scorpio
DEC 7th (11 p.m.) in Sagittarius

2000

JAN 6th (6 p.m.) in Capricorn
FEB 5th (1 p.m.) in Aquarius
MARCH 6th (5 a.m.) in Pisces
APRIL 4th (6 p.m.) in Aries
MAY 4th (4 a.m.) in Taurus
JUNE 2nd (noon) in Gemini
JULY 1st (7 p.m.) in Cancer
JULY 31st (2 a.m.) in Leo
AUG 29th (10 a.m.) in Virgo
SEPT 27th (8 p.m.) in Libra
OCT 27th (8 a.m.) in Scorpio
NOV 25th (11 p.m.) in Sagittarius
DEC 25th (5 p.m.) in Capricorn

The Artist And The Glyphs

Gregory James Kopak was a man inspired by the calling of his heart. As the glyphs made themselves known to him his face was illumined with a childlike joy that comes with inspiration. Gregory would sit watching the sky for long periods of time and then rise to again let pencil, paper and heart bring forth the glyphs. Greg gave birth to eighty-seven glyphs in only ten days.

Gregory James loved God simply. He did not claim to understand why he had been given the gift of these drawings. He simply wanted to do whatever God needed him to do. He died three moths and six days after we met; but not before totally changing my life and all those he touched.

The glyphs are the artful expression of the ancient language of the Sun. They speak to the heart and soul, expressing differently to all. Open your heart to the I AM That I AM and as you observe each glyph and let them speak to your soul.

Greg's beloved

Please send the following:

☐ Mountain Light Newsletter (sample copy- free)

☐ _____ copies of A Day of Grace ($8.95 ea. +$1.00 S&H)

☐ The following discourses: (90 min. channeled cassette tapes)

   $10 each or $29.95 for the album of four, plus $2 per order for S&H

☐ **Tape 1:** Side A: Ascending in Love
   Side B: Meditation Music of the Andes

☐ **Tape 2:** Side A: God in Drag
   Side B: Curriculum in Consciousness

☐ **Tape 3:** Side A: Spiritual Skydiving
   Side B: The Keys to Eden

☐ **Tape 4:** Side A: Love, Fear & Boogeyman Religion
   Side B. Get Up and Go Pee!

☐ Album with all four tapes

   Enclosed: $ _____
   Check or money order only. (Payable to Mountain Light)

   Name _____

   Address _____

   City _____ State _____ Zip _____

   Telephone _____ E-Mail _____

Mountain Light Publishing
PO Box 18909, Asheville, NC 28814.
E-Mail: lightweave@aol.com

About the Author

Michael Lightweaver lives in a secluded cove in the mountains near Asheville, North Carolina, where he is guest master at Mountain Light Sanctuary, a spiritual retreat and nurture center for those seeking a time apart for reflection.